Phil H. LISTEMANN

Colour artwork: Claveworks Graphic

Layout & project design: Phil Listemann

Copyright © Philedition - Phil Listemann 2011

ISBN 978-2-918590-42-2

All rights reserved. No parts of this publication may be reproduced, stored in a retrieval system or transmitted in any form or by any means, electronic, mechanical, photocopying, recording or otherwise, without permission in writing from the Authors.

ACKNOWLEDGEMENTS

Roger Wallsgrove (Text Consultant), Norman Taylor

Edited and printed by Phil H. Listemann

philedition@wanadoo.fr

GLOSSARY OF TERMS

1c, 2c, 3c: First, Second and third Class
AMM: Aviation Machinist's Mate
ACMM: Aviation Chief Machinist's Mate
ACRM: Aviation Chief Radioman
AS: Apprentice Seaman
BAD: Base Air Detachment
BatFor: Battle Force
Cdmr: Commander
Col: Colonel
Del: Delivered

DBR: damaged beyond repair
Ens: Enseign
INA: Inspector of Naval Aviation
Lt (jg): Lieutenant (jg)
NAF: Naval Aircraft Factory
NRAB: Naval Reserve Aviation Base
NAS: Naval Air Station
OH: overhaul
Str.: Stricken from Navy list
TT: Total Time

Curtiss F11C/BFC INTRODUCTION

The XF11C-2 was purchased by the US Navy to become a test aircraft. It is seen here in flight with a 500 lb bomb installed under the fuselage.
(National Archives)

The Curtiss F11C was one of the last attempts by the Curtiss Corporation to remain a major supplier of fighters for the US Navy. For Curtiss, the loss of influence began at the end of the twenties, Boeing then becoming the main supplier of fighters for the USN. Curtiss was still selling aircraft to the USN, mainly observation or training aircraft, and still had good contacts with USN officials, but lacked the prestige of a manufacturer having its own fighters flying in the Navy. It was at the same time a matter of pride and also a marketing point (it is still true today!). But to meet their goal, Curtiss took the easy way, perhaps too easy a way in building a new fighter (XF11C-1) ordered in April 1932. The fighter which received the designation of F11C was actually only an extensive revision of the previous Curtiss fighters sold to the Navy. A new engine, an experimental air-cooled radial Wright SR-1510 fourteen-cylinder twin-row, rated at 600 hp, was installed. The engine drove an unusual (at that time) three-blade propeller allowing it to use a shorter landing gear. Other improvements were also adopted for the new fighter, but even with that the Curtiss F11C cannot be seen as a big step forward.

The first flight occurred in October 1932. Because of continuous overheating problems with the new engine, the propeller was changed for a twin-blade one, and so the landing gear had to be extended. The Curtiss F11C was now a very conventional fighter at a time when aviation was at a turning point, with new technologies and ideas emerging.

Meanwhile, the Navy had purchased another Curtiss product, which became the XF11C-2. This former company demonstrator was in fact older in design, having a radial Wright R-1820 rated at 700 hp and was similar to the production Curtiss Hawk II. This was modified to Navy standard. Both sub-types were destined as dive-bombers from the beginning, being able to carry a 500-lb bomb under the fuselage. In October 1932, USN officials decided to order 28 production F11C-2s, based on the second prototype. The bulk of the order was delivered between March and April 1933.

One existing civil Hawk II (Curtiss demonstrator) purchased by the Navy as test aircraft before to be later modified as XF11C-2 (Bu.No 9213) by contract 26480.

9213
Del 02.05.32; Anacostia 02.05.32; Curtiss 30.05.32; Anacostia 22.06.32; NAS Hampton Roads 24.06.32; Anacostia 07.07.32. Accepted officially by the Navy 07.08.32. DBR 25.08.32. No details available, report not found. **Str-29.09.32.** (74.0 TT)

One prototype of a new fighter XF11C-1 Bu.No 9219 ordered in April 1932 by contract 25572.

9219
Anacostia 19.12.32; Curtiss 15.03.33; officially accepted by the Navy July 1933; Anacostia 10.12.33; Curtiss then Anacostia 29.06.34; INA Paterson 13.10.34; Norfolk 26.11.34; Anacostia 27.02.35; Wright Corp 01.03.35; Anacostia 10.01.36; Langley Field, Norfolk 03.03.39. Obsolete and in need of an OH. Wfu 10.03.39. (319.4 TT). No stricken date.

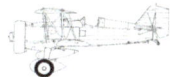

Deliveries and Strenght

Month	Delivered	Total delivered	Acc.	Str.	On Hand
May 32	1	1	-	-	1
.../...					
August 32	-	-	1		-
.../...					
November 32	1	2	-	-	1
December 32	1	3			
.../...					
March 33	10	13	-	-	11
April 33	16	29	-	-	29
.../...					
December 33	-	29	1	-	28
.../...					
April 34	-	29	1	-	27
.../...					
September 34	-	29	1	-	26
.../...					
November 34	-	29	1	-	25
.../...					
September 35	-	29	1	-	24
.../...					
February 36	-	29	1	-	23
.../...					
May 36	-	29	1	-	22
.../...					
July 36	-	29	1	-	21
.../...					
February 37	-	29	1	-	20
.../...					
October 37	-	29	1	-	19
November 37	-	29	1	-	18
.../...					
January 38	-	29	1	-	17
February 38	-	29	1	-	16
.../...					
May 38	-	29	-	2	14
June 38	-	29	-	4	10
.../...					
March 39	-	29	-	1	9
April 39	-	29	-	2	7
.../...					
June 39	-	29	-	4	3
July 39	-	29	-	3	-

Side view of the XF11C-1 Bu.No 9217 which was actually a return to the original Curtiss F6C configuration of 1925 with many state-of-the-art upgrades. That was actually the main weakness of the F11C-1 model, its lack of true innovation. The plane was not bad as such, and rather reliable, but it was at the end of a long improvement process which had reached its limit. That helped to eventually condemn Curtiss few years later. (*SDAM*)

The first production F11C-2 Bu.No 9265 warming up its engine in December 1932 at Norfolk (VA). It is clear of any unit markings. Indeed it spent most of its career as a test aircraft, joining the fleet in 1936. (*Jim Hawkins - Norman Taylor collection*)

TECHNICAL DATA
BFC-2

Manufacturer and production:
30 by Curtiss-Wright Corporation (Buffalo, NY)

Type:
Carrier-borne fighter-bomber.

Accomodation:
One pilot.

Power plant:
One Wright R-1820-78 nine-cylinder radial air-cooled rated 700 hp

Fuel & Oil
Fuel (US Gal):
Main tanks: 94 [355 l]
Auxiliary tank: 52 [197 l]

Oil (US Gal):
Standard: 10.5 [40 l]

Dimensions:
Span (Upper): 31 ft 6-in [9,60 m]
Span (Lower): 26ft 6-in
Length: 25 ft 0-in [7,62 m]
Height: 10 ft 7.25-in [3,20 m]
Wing area: 262 Sq ft [24,35 m²]

Weights:
Empty: 3,111 lb [1 411 kg]
Gross: 4,712 lb [2 136 kg]
4,194 lb [1 902 kg] for the F11C-2

Performance:
Max speed:
198 mph at 4,000 ft
[319 km/h à 700 m]

Crusing speed: 150 mph [241 km/h]

Initial climb: 1,550 ft/min [470 m/min]
1,925 ft/min [585 m/min] for the F11C-2

Service ceiling: 20,700 ft [6 250 m]
24,000 ft [7 300 m] for the F11C-2

Normal range: 560 miles [900 km]

Armament:
2 x fixed forward-firing 0.30-in [7.62 mm] with 500 rpg

provision for:
2 x 116 lb [25 kg] and one 474 lb bombs [100 kg]

Two BFCs flying over San Diego Naval Air Base. Note the bombs racks which can be seen near the roundel.
(*National Archives*)

The green section leader of VF-1B on board F11C-2 Bu.No 9279. The Curtiss F11C existed for a short time, one year only, before becoming the fighter-bomber BFC. Thus photographs showing a F11C-2 in flight are pretty rare. (National Archives)

VF-1B/VF2-B/VB-3
code: 1-F/2-B/3-B
April 1933 - January 1938

The Curtiss F11C began its operational career in May 1933 when VF-1B 'High Hat' took delivery of its first aircraft, replacing its older Boeing F4B-3s. The unit was embarked on USS *Saratoga*, one of the two large USN aircraft carriers in commission at that time. VF-1B flew the two types for a couple of weeks before fully replacing its Boeing fighters. In summer 1933, VF-1B was equipped with 18 F11C-2s, nine arriving in May 1933 (Bu.Nos 9266-9268, 9270, 9272 - 9275), six more in June (Bu.Nos 9276 - 9281) and the last three in mid-July (Bu.Nos 9292, 9331 and 9332). Most of the other aircraft were stored but some were used as test aircraft, like Bu.No 9269 which was modified as the XF11C-3, later becoming the XBF2C-1. Even then, the Curtiss fighter constituted only a tiny part of the USN fighter force as all the other USN fighter units were flying Boeing types. During the first year of service, the F11C appeared to be a safe aircraft, only two F11C-2s were lost by accident. One loss occurred on 12 December 1933, Bu.No 9268 crashing during gunnery practice, killing its pilot, Lt (jg) W.S. Arthur, an experienced pilot with over 900 hours in his log book. The second crash occurred four months later on 13 April 1934 when during a training flight at sea, Enseign A.W. Dunning became short of fuel after being unable to switch to the reserve tank. He had no choice but to to stall his F11C (Bu.No 9281) over the water and there it sank after overturning. The pilot was however safe.

The previous month, in March, Curtiss had sent sets to the USN to modify the F11Cs into BFC-2s, but with the change of role (passing from a true fighter with dive bombing capabilities to a fighter-bomber), the Curtiss fighter suffered a higher attrition rate, around a dozen aircraft being stricken (almost half of the fleet) before the withdrawal of the type in 1939. To identify the new role of VF-1B, the denomination changed to VB-2B on 1 July 1934. If at first attrition remained stable, with the loss of one BFC (Bu.No 9278 on 2 November 1934, pilot safe), and another one in September 1935 (Bu.No 9280, pilot killed), things began to change with three accidents (Bu.Nos 9276, 9272 and 9340), one being fatal, in 1936. The last of these occurred on 4th May, while practicing deck landings; the pilot

An unidentified Curtiss of the last batch parked at San Diego. The colour of the cowling indicates that it was the third aircraft of its section, but the true identity is not known.

The three BFC-2s of the red section of the former VB-2B, Bu.Nos 9339, 9275 and 9337. This photo was taken at San Diego probably in 1937, shortly after the new tail colours had been introduced but with the VB-3 codes yet to be painted on. Note the reverse chevrons painted on the top wings.
(National Archives)

missed his landing on USS *Saratoga* and dived into the water and sank. Attempts to rescue the pilot, Enseign H.N. Boadwee, failed and he sank with his Curtiss, Bu.No 9340. The following year, 1937, was not good either for VB-2B, renamed VB-3 on 1 July 1937, with three more accidents, fortunately with no fatalities (Bu.Nos 9266, 9273 and 9275).

In 1938, the days of the Curtiss BFC were now numbered. From November 1937, the first aircraft had begun to leave the unit and conversion onto the Vought SB2U-1 scout-bomber was well under way. The last Curtisses of VB-3 left in February 1938.

VB-6
code: 6-B
February - June 1938

Nevertheless, the career of the BFC-2 continued for a while, about a dozen BFC-2s being sent to fill the gap in equipping VB-6 'Mountain Goat' of the USS *Enterprise*. VB-6 was waiting for its new aircraft, the Douglas BT-1 dive-bomber and the Curtiss was exactly what the pilots needed for training pending the delivery of their new aircraft. The use of the Curtiss by VB-6 was short, four months only, but was free of any accidents. After June 1938, the Curtisses did not fly much, being used mainly as hack aircraft, but soon cracks appeared in some engine mounts and the last aircraft had to be grounded in 1939 for safety reasons. Contrary to many USN aircraft, it was never used as advanced trainer after its withdrawal from first line units.

In the first part of the thirties, the USN was trying to introduce new fighters and concepts such as the Grumman two-seat FF-1, due to be put into service soon after the F11C appeared and the Curtiss fighter-bomber can be seen as an experiment. No more than one unit was equipped with the F11C/BFC at a time, but it seems that the Curtiss performed well in that role. Nevertheless the concept was short-lived, the category being deleted from the USN list in 1937 after the failure of the BF2C, the successor to the BFC-2 (see part 2). But in any case, by that date, Curtiss had lost out to other manufacturers and the F11C was the last Curtiss fighter to see service with the USN, supplanted then by the major supplier of Navy fighters for a long time, Grumman.

Bu.No 9275 (3-B-18) seen picked up by USS *Holland* one hour after it ditched off San Diego. The salt water prevented any possibility restore the Curtiss to service. Compared to other fighters of its time, the BFC had a rather good safety record. *(National Archives)*

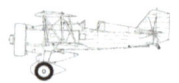

THE REGISTER

Twenty-eight production aircraft F11C-2 ordered in October 1932 by contract 28847 in two batches (9265-9282, 9331-9340). All surviving F11C-2s became BFC-2s in March 1934.

9265

Del 10.11.32; Anacostia 01.12.32; Norfolk 06.12.32; Anacostia 19.01.33; Dahlgren 02.02.33; Anacostia 10.02.33; Curtiss 03.03.33; Norfolk 11.05.33; Curtiss 14.07.33; Norfolk 24.07.33; VF-1B 31.07.33; Anacostia 27.10.33; Dahlgren 08.11.33; NAF 13.02.34; Norfolk 06.03.34; NAF 14.03.34; Wright Aero Corp 11.01.35; San Diego Battle Force 08.02.35; Norfolk Battle Force 18.12.35; San Diego 18.12.35; VB-2B 16.03.36 [*renamed VB-3 on 01.07.37*]; San Diego Battle Force 15.10.37; Norfolk Battle Force 07.01.38; VB-6 17.01.38; Norfolk Battle Force 24.05.38; NAS Seattle 04.06.38. **Str-29.04.39** (1,237.0 TT).

9266

Del 11.03.33; San Diego Battle Force 22.03.33; VF-1B 28.04.33 [*renamed VB-2B on 01.07.34*]; San Diego Battle Force for OH 21.12.34; VB-2B 01.04.35; San Diego Battle Force 18.09.36; VB-2B 18.12.36:
At about 11.00 on 04.02.37, after completing a homing drill and prior to returning to North Island, the pilot, Av.Cad J.J. Lynch, USNR, climbed to an altitude of about 4,500 feet and attempted to roll the plane on top of a loop, from which manoeuvre the plane entered an inverted spin. The direction of rotation of the plane in the spin was not recognised by the pilot. He left the plane with full throttle on, being thrown away. The plane hit the ground in an inverted attitude in a straight flight path at an angle of about 45° to the horizontal. The force of the impact completely demolished the plane and engine. The pilot, with a flying experience of 450.0 hours, landed approximately 100 yards from the wreckage, uninjured.
The plane crashed 16 miles East of Delmar (CA), at 1115. San Diego Battle Force for disposition only, 10.02.37. **Str-30.04.37.** (660.6 TT).

9267

Del 11.03.33; San Diego Battle Force 22.03.33; VF-1B 06.04.33; San Diego 02.03.34; VB-2B 05.12.34; San Diego Battle Force for OH 10.07.36; VB-2B 19.10.36 [*renamed VB-3 on 01.07.37*]; San Diego Battle Force 12.01.38; Norfolk Battle Force 17.01.38; VB-6 18.01.38; Norfolk Battle Force 13.04.38. **Str-31.05.38.** (1,229.0 TT)

9268

Del 18.03.33; San Diego Battle Force 29.03.33; VF-1B 04.05.33.
On 12.12.33 at 11.30, the pilot, Lt (jg) W.S. Arthur, USN, was apparently making a gunnery approach from underneath on a towed sleeve. He started at about the level of the sleeve, dived slightly and pulled up to bear on the sleeve in a tight flipper turn. As he completed his run, he ducked under the sleeve and for some indeterminate reason headed down for the water in a 45° dive at about 120° to the left of the base course of towing plane. The plane never recovered from this dive and struck the water in a slight right turn at high speed. The pilots of this accompanying planes could see no attempt on the part of Lt Arthur to jump clear. Just before striking the water the nose came up slightly as if an effort were being made to pull out of the dive. The plane sank instantly carrying the pilot with it 6 miles off La Jolla (CA).
Arthur's body was never recovered. He was an experienced pilot, having logged over 900 flying hours. **Str-31.01.34.** (117.85 TT)

9269

Prototype of the XF11C-3 (XBF2C-1). See BF2C-1 part.

9270

Del 18.03.33; San Diego Battle Force 29.03.33; VF-1B 11.05.33; San Diego 28.03.34; INA (Wright Corp) 30.10.34; NAF 11.11.35; San Diego Battle Force for OH 07.04.36; NAF 17.06.36; San Diego Battle Force 28.02.37; VB-2B 01.03.37 [*renamed VB-3 on 01.07.37*]; San Diego Battle Force 14.03.38; Pearl Harbor FAB 14.03.38. **Str-30.06.39.** (707.6 TT).

9271

Del 24.03.33; San Diego Battle Force 06.04.33; VF-1B 12.05.33 [*renamed VB-2B on 01.07.34*]; San Diego Battle Force for OH 22.11.34; VB-2B 06.03.35; San Diego Battle Force for OH 15.09.36; VB-2B 08.12.36 [*renamed VB-3 on 01.07.37*]; San Diego Battle Force 27.01.38; Norfolk Battle Force 08.02.38; VB-6 08.02.38; Norfolk Battle Force 19.05.38. **Str-30.06.38.** (1,259.8 TT)

Bu.No 9265 spent a large part of its career as test aircraft. However, it was briefly used by operational squadrons during that time, probably to test various equipment. It was briefly used by VF-1B in 1933, later returning to the squadron (now VF-2B) which became VB-3 on 1 July 1937. The red tail was changed for a white tail, but for a very short time, the BFC-2s continued to wear the codes '2-B' instead of '3-B', giving a clue to when this picture was taken, probably in July 1937. The cowling has the markings for third aircraft of the Fifth section - Green.
(*National Archives*)

Bu.No 9266 seen shortly after it had been converted to a BFC. The mechanics have altered the denomination from 'F11C-2' to 'BFC-2' on the tail.
Knowing that VF-1B became VB-2B on 01.07.34 and the first conversion kits were installed in March 1934, this photo was probably taken during spring 1934, as the codes of VF-1B are still worn. The tail is red (USS Saratoga) and it is the aircraft of the leader of the First section, with the engine cowling and fuselage band in red. Note the gunnery trophy painted ahead of the cockpit. On the upper wing the red chevron with the black '1' inside can been seen in the normal position, believe to be the rule for F11Cs.
(*National Archives*)

The reason why the tail of Bu.No 9266 was painted in white is not known, but it should be red, as 9266 was lost in February 1937 before the change of tail colour in July when the USS Saratoga adopted this colour for her aircraft. This mistake may have occurred during an overhaul or repairs. Note the absence of the bomb racks which could suggest a recent stay at San Diego Battle Force facilities. As second aircraft of the Fourth section, the upper half of the cowling is black.
(*National Archives*)

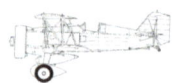

9272

Del 24.03.33; San Diego Battle Force 06.04.33; VF-1B 19.05.33; San Diego Battle Force 27.03.34; VB-2B 16.11.34; San Diego Battle Force 21.02.36.

On 29 July 1936, ACMM H.H. Pavlet was preparing a test flight from NAS San Diego. After taking off, the pilot gained altitude to about 3,500 feet, checking the performances of the plane, engine and instruments. Everything being normal, he began to execute a slow roll. Upon reaching a position between one half and three-fourths of the way to inverted flight, the engine coughed and cut out, a strong rush of gasoline began to gush forth from somewhere forward. The quantity being such that he had the impression of it being pumped out under pressure. This was followed immediately by the fire which he is positive he first noted in the vicinity of the floorboards forward. This flame developed into a burst of flame which enveloped the plane approaching the nature of an explosion. The above sequence of events was so rapid that they were almost simultaneous. Pilot left the plane immediately and the plane crashed to e complete wreck in the Bay at 13.50, local time, being still in flames upon impact with the water.

H.H. Pavlet was safe but had burns on face, arms, hands and shoulders. He had logged over 2,200 of flying time. **Str-31.08.36** (535.4 TT)

9273

Del 30.03.33; San Diego Battle Force 12.04.33; VF-1B 16.05.33 [*renamed VB-2B on 01.07.34*]; San Diego Battle Force for OH 03.12.34; VB-2B 01.04.35; San Diego Battle Force for OH 28.10.36; VB-2B 12.01.37 [*renamed VB-3 on 01.07.37*].

On 08.10.37, the pilot, inexperienced in this type, took off at 05.12 for a night training flight from NAS San Diego. His take off was performed in very turbulent air caused by previous aircraft of his squadron. About five seconds after commencing the take-off, the plane swerved toward the section leader. The right wing dropped, the pilot cut the throttle and switch and applied left brake. The plane turned over once to the left, and skidded several feet on its back.

Pilot, Lt (Jr) C.C. Gold safe, had logged 409.5 hours in the air, only 67.2 in Fighters. Damaged beyond repair. **Str-30.11.37**. (945.9 TT).

9274

Del 30.03.33; San Diego Battle Force 13.04.33; VF-1B 23.05.33; San Diego Battle Force 26.03.34; VB-2B 12.12.34; San Diego Battle Force for OH 17.07.36; VB-2B 15.10.36 [*renamed VB-3 on 01.07.37*]; San Diego Battle Force 27.01.38; Norfolk Battle Force 07.02.38; VB-6 07.02.38; Norfolk Battle Force 19.05.38. **Str-30.06.38** (1,098.3 TT).

9275

Del 31.03.33; San Diego Battle Force 12.04.33; VF-1B 24.05.34 [*renamed VB-2B on 01.07.34*]; San Diego Battle Force for OH 12.04.35; VB-2B 05.08.35; San Diego Battle Force 25.01.37; VB-2B 02.04.37 [*renamed VB-3 on 01.07.37*]; San Diego Battle Force 16.11.37.

On 15 November 1937 at 14.30, during the approach of a gunnery run the pilot noticed that the engine revolutions were dropping off considerably. Upon opening the throttle the engine appeared to turn momentarily, then back fired and dropped off rather rapidly. At this time all instruments were checked and found to be operating normally. Then, the pilot notified the senior officer present and headed for North Island. Approximately 5 miles off shore he found that he did not have sufficient power to stay in the air, and he made a full stall landing in the water. The plane did not nose over, and was picked up approximately 45 minutes later by the USS Holland. It was further transferred to the USS *Robin*, for return to North Island. The flotation gear functioned normally.

The trailing edge of the rudder was the only part damaged during salvage operations. The plane on previous hops (2 hours) on this day with the same pilot had functioned perfectly. The crashed occurred, 10 miles bearing 240° True from DelMar, (CA). The pilot, AC W.A. Gates, USNR, was safe and had logged 415 hours of flying time.. No details as such are given on why the aircraft was stricken, but it is seems that the fact that the aircraft was immersed in salt water during about one hour, would have obliged the Navy to clean up the Curtiss. Considering the age and the number of hours flown by the fuselage, it seems that it was not worthwhile **Str-31.12.37** (1,119.2 TT)

9276

Del 31.03.33; San Diego Battle Force 01.04.33; VF-1B 31.05.33 [*renamed VB-2B on 01.07.34*]; San Diego Battle Force for OH 02.03.35; VB-2B 18.04.35; San Diego Battle Force 02.03.36.

On 28.02.36, during a night training flight from NAS San Diego, the pilot, Lt (jg) L.W. Mang, USN, made a left turn over Army hangars, South Field, to begin first approach for night field carrier landings. His indicated altitude at that time about 275 ft. He put his plane in an approach attitude and started to slip off enough altitude to be about 150 ft upon getting squared away in the groove and picking up the signal officer. Just as he thought this position had been reached (indicated altitude 150 ft) his plane made contact with the ground; it bounced into the air; he gave the engine a burst of gas and placed the plane in a stalled attitude by pulling vigorously back on the stick and at the same time levelling the wings. When the plane landed again, it skidded along on the ground with the left wing down. It started nosing over rapidly and he reached for the buckle on the safety belt. When the plane was about one-half the way over, he was thrown clear of the plane. It was 21.25. Lt (jg) Mang was safe having sustained minor injuries only. His log book had recorded 398.5 hours at that time. **Str-31.03.38** (578.4 TT).

9277
Del 03.04.33; San Diego Battle Force 20.04.33; VF-1B 05.06.33 [*renamed VB-2B on 01.07.34*]; San Diego Battle Force for OH 25.02.35; VB-2B 19.04.35; San Diego Battle Force for OH 14.12.36; VB-2B 01.03.37 [*renamed VB-3 on 01.07.37*]; San Diego Battle Force for OH 20.12.37; Pearl Harbor FAB 16.06.38. **Str-30.06.39** (1,231.6 TT)

9278
Del 05.04.33; San Diego Battle Force 20.04.33; VF-1B 08.06.33 [*renamed VB-2B on 01.07.34*];
While making a dive bombing attack, on 02.11.34, the pilot noticed a quantity of gasoline flowing into the cockpit. This was accompanied by a loss of fuel pressure and stoppage of the engine at about 2,500 feet altitude. The pressure could not be regained by shifting suction to either tank nor by using the hand pump. At the completion of the pull out, about 1,500 feet altitude, the pilot, Lt (jg) L.L. Koepke, USN, continued to gain altitude until he had lost all excess speed. He then glided the plane down and levelled off and stalled it as for a normal landing. On landing the plane nosed up a small amount but settled to a normal position immediately. As soon as the pilot released himself from his quick releasing parachute he stood up in the seat and pulled the flotation release. He watched the bags fill up and then turned around to get his life raft out of the compartment. He unlocked the compartment door and was pulling on the raft when the plane sank from underneath him. It was 09.30 local time. he hung to the right flotation bag which had broken loose and was picked upon few minutes later by the USS *Oklahoma*.
Koepke was an experienced pilot with close of 1,000 hours logged. **Str-31.01.35** (240.4 TT)

9279
Del 07.04.33; San Diego Battle Force 20.04.33; VF-1B 12.06.33 [*renamed VB-2B on 01.07.34*]; San Diego Battle Force for OH 18.06.35; VB-2B 06.09.35; San Diego Battle Force for OH 07.06.37; VB-3 10.08.37; San Diego Battle Force 12.01.38.
Crashed on take-off from Wilmer field (TX) to NAS Norfolk on 14.01.38 at 1630. The field was not a regular landing field and was rough with brushes and weeds covering most of it. The plane struck large bush and went over on its back causing the plane to be practically a complete wreck.
Pilot AvCdt F.R. Kerr, USNR, safe with almost 1,000 hours logged. **Str-30.04.38** (1,265.1 TT)

9280
Del 07.04.33; San Diego Battle Force 20.04.33; VF-1B 15.06.33 [*renamed VB-2B on 01.07.34*]; San Diego Battle Force for OH 21.12.34; VB-2B 12.04.35; San Diego Battle Force 01.10.35. Report found but it is totally illegible. However fleet air officials announced at that time that on 16.09.35:
Lieutenant Charles Keith Palmer, 27, navy flier, was killed today when his single-seater fighting plane failed to come out of a mile-high dive and crashed at Border field, San Diego. The flier, attempting a dive-bombing maneuver, went into the fatal spin at an altitude of 5,000 Feet. **Str-30.11.35** (402.7 TT).

9281
Del 11.04.33; San Diego Battle Force 27.04.33; VF-1B 26.06.33.
During a training flight at sea, on 13.04.34 at 1215 off USS *Saratoga* at sea the pilot, Ensign A.W. Dunnings, USNR, shifted from auxiliary tank believing it to be nearly empty. The shifting procedure was correct, however, as soon as he turned his selector valve his engine spurt and failed. The gasoline supply was shifted to reserve and the hand pump used to not avail. The plane was landed fully stalled, slightly out of the wind and it immediately turned over on its back. After extricating himself the pilot had to dive under water to pull the flotation gear which functioned normally. Due to the inverted position of the plane, the flotation bags, instead of pushing up on the upper wing were pulling against the plane's weight. The strength of their lashings proved inadequate and they were ripped off. The plane sank immediately. The pilot was unable to get his rubber boat out of its stowage under the old style turtleback in the short time available before the plane sank. It is the opinion of the board that the forced landing was caused by the improper functioning of the fuel system or carburetor.
Pilot safe. Dunning was had a fying experience of over 500 hours, 123 of which on F-11C. **Str-31.08.34**. (168.65 TT).

9282
Del 11.04.33; San Diego Battle Force 27.04.33; VF-1B 10.07.33 [*renamed VB-2B on 01.07.34*]; San Diego Battle Force for OH 02.07.35; VB-2B 07.10.35; San Diego Battle Force for OH 04.12.35; VB-2B 18.03.36 [*renamed VB-3 on 01.07.37*]; San Diego Battle Force for OH 25.08.37; VB-3 05.11.37; San Diego Battle Force for repair after a minor accident 17.12.37; Pearl Harbor FAB 16.06.38. **Str-30.06.39.** (1,042.8 TT)

9331
Del 13.04.33; San Diego Battle Force 27.04.33; VF-1B 14.07.33 [*renamed VB-2B on 01.07.34*]; San Diego Battle Force for OH 21.01.35; VB-2B 16.04.35; San Diego Battle Force for OH 20.11.36; VB-2B 08.02.37 [*renamed VB-3 on 01.07.37*]; San Diego Battle Force 14.01.38; Norfolk Battle Force 02.02.38; VB-6 02.02.38; Norfolk Battle Force 13.04.38. **Str-31.05.38** (1,192.5 TT).

Bu.No 9268 was the only F11C-2 not to have been converted to BFC standard, having been destroyed in an accident in December 1933. This photo may have been taken before its delivery to the US Navy, as the markings are not fully painted on. Indeed, the cowling remains unpainted because it should have its lower half part painted in red as being the third aircraft of the first section. Also, as far as available photographs can testify, the F11C-2s of VF-1B were wearing the gunnery trophy ahead of the cockpit, missing on this F11C-2.
(*National Archives*)

During its service with VB-2B on the USS *Saratoga* (red tail), Bu.No 9272 was the mount of the leader of the Third section with a blue engine cowling and blue band, white outlined. It was later lost during a test flight in July 1936, after an overhaul.
(*National Archives*)

Bu.No 9274 was sent for overhaul in July 1936. When it returned to VB-2B the following October it became the second aircraft of the Fifth section with its upper half engine cowling painted in Willow Green. In February 1938, it was one of the few which were used by the VB-6 and was one of the last to fly with the US Navy.
(*National Archives*)

Bu.No 9282 whilst in service with VF-1B in 1933. It was used by the leader of the Sixth section, with a Lemon Yellow band on the fuselage and its engine cowling fully painted in the same colour. Note the gunnery trophy pennant painted ahead of the cockpit.
(*National Archives*)

Bu.No 9282 was the last F11C-2 of the initial batch taken on charge by VF-1B. Thus, it became 1-F-18 as being the third aircraft of the Sixth section with its lower engine cowling painted in Lemon Yellow, Black outlined. Note the Gunnery Trophy pennant which was painted on both sides of the fuselage. 9282 is seen soon after its conversion to a BFC-2 but before VF1-B was renamed VB-2B in July 1934.
(*National Archives*)

Bu.No 9334 seen after 1 July 1937, when the 'High Hat' Squadron became VB-3 on the USS *Saratoga* with a new white tail. This BFC-2 is the second aircraft of the Sixth section, with the upper half cowling painting in yellow, outlined with a thin black band. Bu.No. 9334 left the 'High Hat' Squadron in the following October.

9332
Del 13.04.33; San Diego Battle Force 27.04.33; VF-1B 17.07.33 [*renamed VB-2B on 01.07.34*]; San Diego Battle Force 24.06.35; VB-2B 12.09.35; San Diego Battle Force 06.10.36, VB-2B 28.12.36 [*renamed VB-3 on 01.07.37*]; San Diego Battle Force 20.01.38; Norfolk Battle Force 05.02.38; VB-6 07.02.38; Norfolk Battle Force 06.06.38. **St-30.06.38**. (1,475.8 TT)

9333
Del 14.04.33; San Diego Battle Force 27.04.33; VF-1B 14.12.33 [*renamed VB-2B on 01.07.34*]; SO Saratoga 16.04.34; Norfolk Battle Force for OH 23.07.34; VB-2B 07.09.34; San Diego Battle Force for OH 19.02.35; VB-2B 19.07.35; San Diego Battle Force 19.11.35, VB-2B 04.03.36 [*renamed VB-3 on 01.07.37*]; San Diego Battle Force for OH 20.09.37; VB-3 09.12.37; San Diego Battle Force 19.01.38; Norfolk Battle Force 05.02.38; VB-6 07.02.38; Norfolk Battle Force 24.05.38; NAS Seattle 04.06.38. Grounded 28.11.38 (Various cracks found on engine mounts). **St-29.04.39** (1,124.5 TT).

9334
Del 14.04.33; San Diego Battle Force 27.04.33; VF-1B 14.02.34 [*renamed VB-2B on 01.07.34*]; SO Saratoga 16.04.34, Norfolk Battle Force for OH 23.07.34; VB-2B 10.09.34; San Diego Battle Force for OH 29.01.36; VB-2B 20.04.36 [*renamed VB-3 on 01.07.37*]; San Diego Battle Force for OH 25.10.37; Pear Harbor FAB 14.03.38. **Str-30.06.39** (1,020.4 TT).

9335
Del 18.04.33; San Diego Battle Force 05.05.33; VB-2B 23.02.34 [*renamed VB-2B on 01.07.34*]; San Diego Battle Force for OH 05.09.35; VB-2B 19.02.36 [*renamed VB-3 on 01.07.37*]; San Diego Battle Force for OH 15.09.37; VB-3 22.11.37; San Diego Battle Force 19.01.38; Norfolk Battle Force 21.02.38; VB-6 21.02.38; Norfolk Battle Force 25.05.38; FAB Coco Solo 20.07.38. Grounded 14.06.39 (cracks on engine mounts). **Str-31.07.39** (1,107.9 TT).

9336
Del 19.04.33; San Diego Battle Force 05.05.33; VF-1B 27.02.34 [*renamed VB-2B on 01.07.34*]; Grumman date unknown then Norfolk 13.07.34; VB2-B date unknown; San Diego Battle Force for OH 26.09.35; VB-2B 26.02.36; San Diego Battle Force for OH 14.12.36; VB-2B 24.03.37 [*renamed VB-3 on 01.07.37*]; San Diego Battle Force 14.01.38; Norfolk Battle Force 02.02.38; VB-6 02.02.38; Norfolk Battle Force 01.06.38. Assigned to FAB Coco Solo but order cancelled. **Str-30.06.38** (1,072.8 TT).

9337
Del 22.04.33; San Diego Battle Force 05.05.33; VF-1B 27.02.34 [*renamed VB-2B on 01.07.34*]; Grumman date unknown then Norfolk 13.07.34; VB2-B date unknown; San Diego Battle Force for OH 16.10.35; VB-2B 26.02.36 [*renamed VB-3 on 01.07.37*]; San Diego Battle Force for OH 17.08.37; VB-3 25.10.37; San Diego Battle Force 27.01.38.
During a ferry flight on 02.02.38, the aircraft landed at Tuscon (AZ) under conditions of light and variable winds. After a short run, the plane started to the right and the pilot applied left brake with apparently no effect. The turn continued until the castering tail wheel disengaged and permitted the plane to turn sharply to the right which resulted in the plane striking the ground with its left wing and then catapulted over on its back. The center section and cabane struts collapsed causing the pilot to be cut about the face and head by the windshield.
It was 13.15, local time. 02.02.38 at 1315, Tuscon Airfield (AZ). Pilot, AvCdt K. Armistead, safe. Aircraft damaged beoynd repair. Kirk Armistead, was the same pilot who was flying F2A-3 BuAer 01562/MF-13 and was leading section 3 as Captain of VMF-221 during the Battle of Midway. He was shot down but safe on the only major air battle the F2A was involved in with the Marines during the war on 04.06.42. He claimed on Type 99 dive bomber probable that day. At the time of the accident, he had logged over 500 hours of flying time, 230 on fighter planes. **Str-28.02.38** (944.0 TT).

9338
Del 22.04.33; San Diego Battle Force 05.05.33; VB-2B 09.03.34; San Diego Battle Force for OH 18.09.35; VB-2B 19.02.36 [*renamed VB-3 on 01.07.37*]; San Diego Battle Force for OH 02.08.37; VB-3 01.10.37; San Diego battle Force 27.01.38; Norfolk Battle Force 05.02.38; VB-6 07.02.38; Norfolk Battle Force 25.02.38; FAB Coco Solo 20.07.38. Grounded 14.06.39. **Str-31.07.39** (1,186.1 TT).

9339
Del 27.04.33; San Diego Battle Force 12.05.33; VB-2B 13.03.34; San Diego Battle Force for OH 16.08.35; VB-2B 13.02.36; accident - San Diego Battle Force 21.02.36. Repaired and ROS; VB-2B 20.07.36; Crashed 20.06.37 then San Diego Battle Force for OH and repaired 24.06.37; Norfolk Battle Force 30.09.37; San Diego Battle Force 06.01.38; Norfolk Battle Force 17.01.38; VB-6 17.01.38; Norfolk Battle Force 25.05.38; FAB Coco Solo 20.07.38. Grounded 14.06.39. **Str-31.07.39** (940.3 TT).

9340
Del 27.04.33; San Diego Battle Force 12.05.33; Norfolk Battle Force 16.07.34; VB-2B date unknown; San Diego Battle Force for

OH 10.01.36; VB-2B 31.03.36.

Pilot Ensign H.N. Boadwee, USNR, made an approach for a landing on board of USS *Saratoga*, 04.05.36. Lt (jg) Thoms B. Payne, USN, was standing on the flight deck about fifty feet forward barrier observing the approach at the time. The down wind part of the approach prior to the turn into the 'groove' was quite close aboard, approximately 500 feet outboard of the ship, necessitating a sharp 180° turn to get into the 'groove'. Although the plane was banked steeply it crossed the stern of the Saratoga to the starboard side. Evidently realising he had crosses too far over, the pilot banked still more steeply. Immediately thereafter the plane dove into the water astern of the *Saratoga* at an angle of about 70° to the horizontal. As observer could not see the plane after it passed below the level of the flight deck, he is unable to state the actual attitude of the plane on making contact with the water. As soon as the airplane disappeared from his sight, he ran aft to a point about 50 feet abaft the after turret on the starboard side of the ship. From there, he could see either one wing or a portion of the tail surfaces sticking out of water for a period of not more than twenty seconds. The plane sank practically immediately and after the tail had submerged nothing was left floating on the surface.

It was 0850, local time. Pilot Ensign H.N. Boadwee, USNR, with over 450 hours already logged was killed. **Str-30.06.36** (450.6 TT)

Bu.No 9331 was issued to VF-1B in July 1933 and became the second aircraft of the Sixth Section (1-F-17). So its upper half engine cowling was painted in Lemon Yellow with a thin black band at its base. In July 1934, the codes were altered to 2-B-17 and new denomination painted on the tail, without any other changes. In January 1935, it was sent to San Diego Battle Force to be overhauled, so we can easily guess that this photo was taken before that date.

Bu.No 9332 was issued to VF-1B three days after 9331 in July 1933 and became the third aircraft of the Sixth Section (1-F-18). So its lower half engine cowling was painted in Lemon Yellow with a thin black band at its top. In July 1934, the codes were altered to 2-B-18 and new denomination painted on the tail, without any other changes. In January 1935, it was sent to San Diego Battle Force probably for overhaul, so we can easily guess that this photo was taken before that date.

Bu.No 9333 seen during summer 1937. From 1 July 1937 onwards, VB-2B became VB-3 after the major changes which occurred in the US Navy at the same date. Aircraft of the leader of the Third section, it had the fuselage band painted in True Blue (White outlined), and the engine cowling was also painted in blue. Note the white 'C' painted behind the 'High Hat' awarded for proficiency in communications. This marking appeared after the 1935-1936 communication competition.
(*National Archives*)

When VB-3 began to receive the Vought SB2U, Bu.No 9333 was sent to storage at San Diego in January 1938, but for a short time only. Indeed, it belongs to the small batch which was taken on charge by VB-6 (USS *Enterprise*) in February that year as stopgap waiting for their BT-1s. In May it eventually left VB-6 and was grounded before the end of year after various cracks had been found in the engine mounts. As second aircraft of the Sixth section, the upper cowling is painting in Lemon Yellow with a thin black band.
(*National Archives*)

Stored at first, Bu.No 9338 was taken on charge by VB-2B in March 1934 at the time the conversion sets were sent to the unit, meaning that it probably flew just a couple of hours as an F11C-2 before arriving already converted to a BFC-2. At that time it became the third aircraft of the First section, with the lower half of its engine cowling painted in red. However, it is rather difficult to know when this photo was taken as 9338 three times left the unit and returned four times between August 1935 and June 1937. The codes may have been changed at each return. Note the chevron in normal position and the individual number painted on the top wing, also visible on '2-B-1' in front of 9338
(*National Archives*)

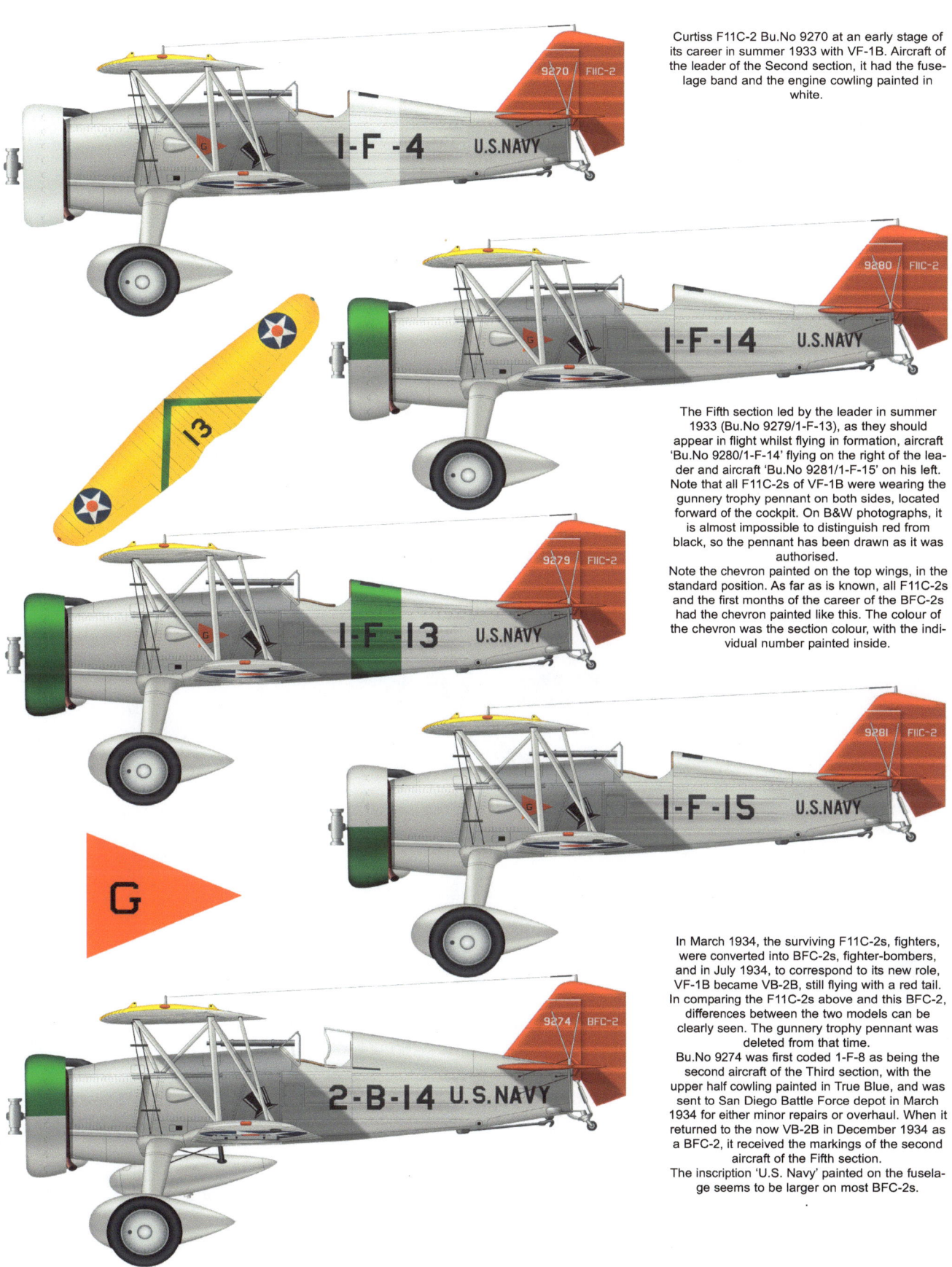

Curtiss F11C-2 Bu.No 9270 at an early stage of its career in summer 1933 with VF-1B. Aircraft of the leader of the Second section, it had the fuselage band and the engine cowling painted in white.

The Fifth section led by the leader in summer 1933 (Bu.No 9279/1-F-13), as they should appear in flight whilst flying in formation, aircraft 'Bu.No 9280/1-F-14' flying on the right of the leader and aircraft 'Bu.No 9281/1-F-15' on his left. Note that all F11C-2s of VF-1B were wearing the gunnery trophy pennant on both sides, located forward of the cockpit. On B&W photographs, it is almost impossible to distinguish red from black, so the pennant has been drawn as it was authorised.
Note the chevron painted on the top wings, in the standard position. As far as is known, all F11C-2s and the first months of the career of the BFC-2s had the chevron painted like this. The colour of the chevron was the section colour, with the individual number painted inside.

In March 1934, the surviving F11C-2s, fighters, were converted into BFC-2s, fighter-bombers, and in July 1934, to correspond to its new role, VF-1B became VB-2B, still flying with a red tail. In comparing the F11C-2s above and this BFC-2, differences between the two models can be clearly seen. The gunnery trophy pennant was deleted from that time.
Bu.No 9274 was first coded 1-F-8 as being the second aircraft of the Third section, with the upper half cowling painted in True Blue, and was sent to San Diego Battle Force depot in March 1934 for either minor repairs or overhaul. When it returned to the now VB-2B in December 1934 as a BFC-2, it received the markings of the second aircraft of the Fifth section.
The inscription 'U.S. Navy' painted on the fuselage seems to be larger on most BFC-2s.

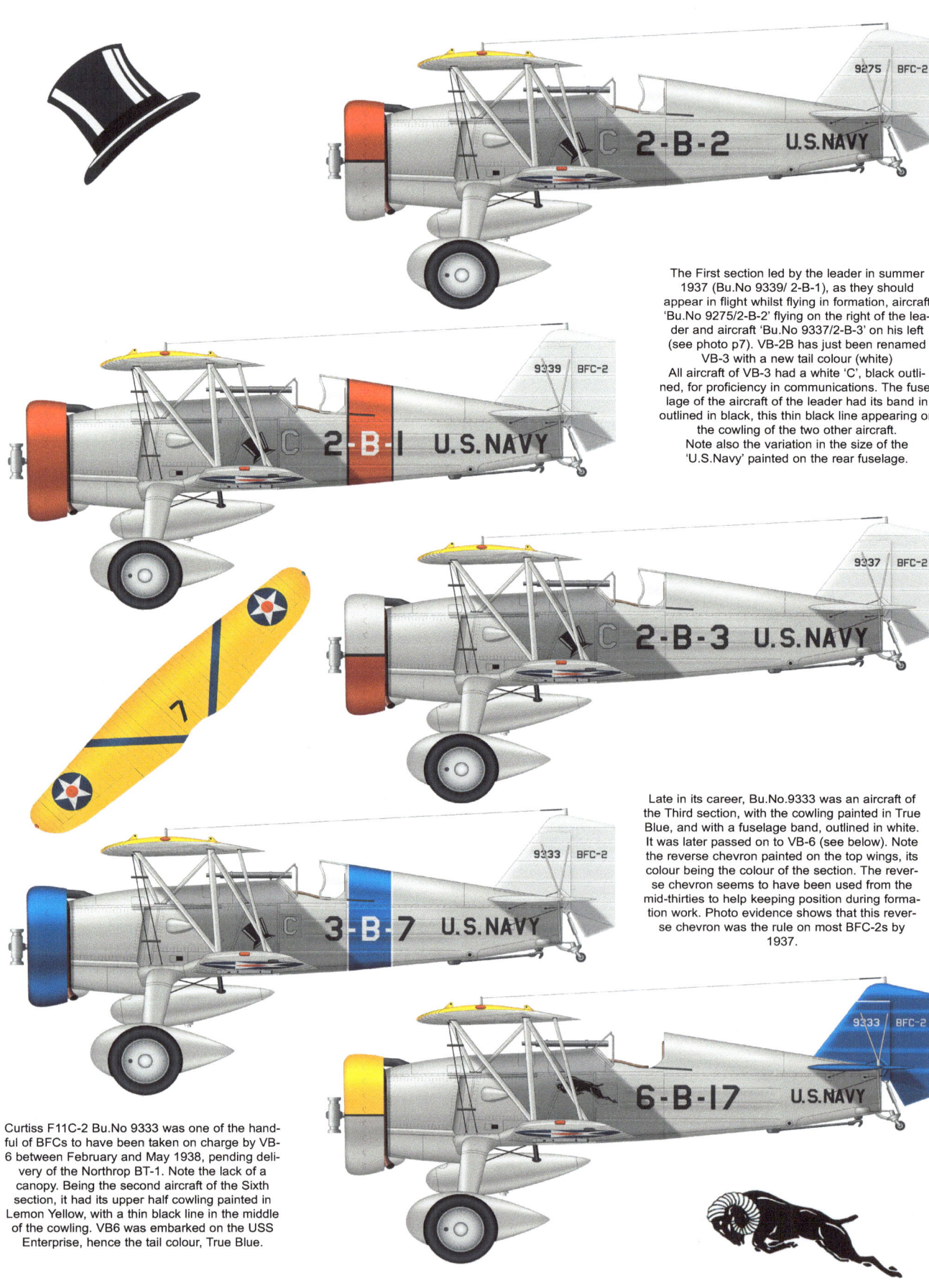

The First section led by the leader in summer 1937 (Bu.No 9339/ 2-B-1), as they should appear in flight whilst flying in formation, aircraft 'Bu.No 9275/2-B-2' flying on the right of the leader and aircraft 'Bu.No 9337/2-B-3' on his left (see photo p7). VB-2B has just been renamed VB-3 with a new tail colour (white)
All aircraft of VB-3 had a white 'C', black outlined, for proficiency in communications. The fuselage of the aircraft of the leader had its band in outlined in black, this thin black line appearing on the cowling of the two other aircraft.
Note also the variation in the size of the 'U.S.Navy' painted on the rear fuselage.

Late in its career, Bu.No.9333 was an aircraft of the Third section, with the cowling painted in True Blue, and with a fuselage band, outlined in white. It was later passed on to VB-6 (see below). Note the reverse chevron painted on the top wings, its colour being the colour of the section. The reverse chevron seems to have been used from the mid-thirties to help keeping position during formation work. Photo evidence shows that this reverse chevron was the rule on most BFC-2s by 1937.

Curtiss F11C-2 Bu.No 9333 was one of the handful of BFCs to have been taken on charge by VB-6 between February and May 1938, pending delivery of the Northrop BT-1. Note the lack of a canopy. Being the second aircraft of the Sixth section, it had its upper half cowling painted in Lemon Yellow, with a thin black line in the middle of the cowling. VB6 was embarked on the USS Enterprise, hence the tail colour, True Blue.

18

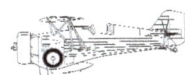

Curtiss BF2C
INTRODUCTION

F11C-2 Bu.No 9269 was chosen to become the prototype XF11C-3. After successful trials, an order for 27 F11C-3s was placed, soon renamed BF2C-1 before delivery.

When the F11C became available, progress was underway in many ways fro the type. Among them, was the retractable gear. Curtiss was not the pioneer in this field, but had no choice but to include such an improvement in its next fighter if it wanted to remain in the race. Logically, Curtiss started working on this project from its last fighter in productions, the Curtiss F11C/BFC. The fifth production airframe was modified to become the XF11C-3 using a system developed by Grumman and first installed in the Grumman FF-1. Although heavier than the F11C-2 with the new system, and using the same engine, the XF11C-3 which first flew in April 1933 was faster. The first results were rather encouraging, testing continuing until the loss of the prototype in September 1934. Meanwhile, the XF11C-3 had become the XBF2C-1 in March 1934 and not XBFC-3, the changes having been considering as major enough to add a digit to the designation.

For the Navy, the tests were satisfactory and, logically, an order was placed in Spring 1934 to equip one squadron plus spares, at that time still under the designation of F11C-3. Only two major internal changes were made on the production aircraft, the first being the wings, which used the metal framework of the XF11C-1 and a new aerofoil. The variant of the engine chosen was the Wright R-1820-04 of 700 hp driving a controllable-pitch propeller. But for Curtiss it was far from a total success as at the same time the Navy ordered 54 Grumman F2F-1s to defend the aircraft carriers of the fleet, the Curtiss model being seen as an improved version of the Curtiss BFC-2, but not as a new fighter.

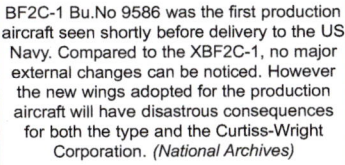

BF2C-1 Bu.No 9586 was the first production aircraft seen shortly before delivery to the US Navy. Compared to the XBF2C-1, no major external changes can be noticed. However the new wings adopted for the production aircraft will have disastrous consequences for both the type and the Curtiss-Wright Corporation. *(National Archives)*

9269

Del 27.05.33 as XF11C-3; Anacostia 27.05.33; Norfolk 09.06.33; Anacostia 17.06.33; Curtiss 05.07.33; Anacostia 23.09.33; Norfolk (Experimental Department) 11.10.33; Anacostia 13.10.33; Curtiss 25.10.33; Anacostia 01.11.33; Curtiss 07.12.33 [became XBF2C-1 in March 1934]; Anacostia 31.07.34; Norfolk (Experimental Department) 10.08.34.

On 18.09.34, While taking off, the engine cut out when the plane was at an altitude of about 200 ft. The pilot landed the plane in the shallow water of a branch creek of Little Inlet. The plane landed fully stalled with the wheels down. Upon impact with the water the plane turned over on its back and rested on the mud bottom. It was 10.15. Investigation disclosed the following salient facts, that the engine failed due to lose of fuel suction; that the pilot had been in the air for one hour and 55 minutes, performing normal aerobatics and gunnery maneuvers, completing these with several landings in Auxiliary Field #2. At the time of the engine failure the gasoline valve was set on 'main', the quantity gauge indicated approximately thirty gallons and actually 32.25 gallons were drained from the tank on recovery. No gasoline was lost from the tank. Upon recovery of the fuselage investigation showed that fuel suction would be lost from the main tank with the plane climbing in the 3 point attitude with the quantity of fuel remaining in the tank. Th pilot did not shift to reserve and it is doubtful weather fuel suction would have been regained with altitude he had at the time of the failure.

Pilot, Lt (jg) W.C. Kaiser, USN, safe, was an experienced pilot with 750 flying gime logged including about 6 on the aircraft. **Str-31.10.34.** (253.75 TT)

DELIVERIES AND STRENGHT

Month	Delivered	Total delivered	Acc.	Str.	On Hand
March 34	1	1	-	-	**1**
.../...					
September 34	-	-	1	-	**-**
October 34	2	3	-	-	**2**
November 34	25	28	-	-	**27**
.../...					
January 35	-	28	1	-	**26**
.../...					
August 35	-	28	1	-	**25**
September 35	-	28	1	-	**24**
October 35	-	28	1	-	**23**
.../...					
January 36	-	28	-	1	**22**
.../...					
February 37	-	28	-	19	**3**
.../...					
April 37	-	28	-	1	**2**
June 37	-	28	-	1	**1**
.../..					
November 39	-	28	-	1	**-**

TECHNICAL DATA
BF2C-1

Manufacturer and production:
30 by Curtiss-Wright Corporation (Buffalo, NY)

Type:
Carrier-borne fighter-bomber.

Accomodation:
One pilot.

Power plant:
One Wright R-1820-04 nine-cylinder radial air-cooled rated 700 hp

Fuel & Oil
Fuel (US Gal):
Main tanks: 110 [415 l]
Auxiliary tank: 60 [227 l]

Oil (US Gal):
Standard: 13.0 [49 l]

Dimensions:
Span (Upper): 31 ft 6-in [9,60 m]
Span (Lower): 26ft 6-in
Length: 24 ft 4-in [7,41 m]

Height : 9 ft 11.05-in [3,03 m]
Wing area : 262 Sq ft [24,35 m²]

Weights:
Empty: 3,326 lb [1 509 kg]
Gross: 4,552 lb [2 065 kg]

Performance:
Max speed:
225 mph at 8,000 ft
[362 km/h à 1 400 m]

Crusing speed: 157 mph [253 km/h]
Initial climb: 1,950 ft/min [590 m/min]
Service ceiling: 27,000 ft [8 250 m]
Normal range: 725 miles [1,170 km]

Armament:
2 x fixed forward-firing 0.30-in [7.62 mm] with 500 rpg

provision for:
2 x 116 lb [25 kg] and one 474 lb bombs [100 kg]

The First section of VB-5B in flight shortly after the introduction of the type into US Navy inventory. Unexpected problems put an premature end to its career, and the BF2C-1 can also been seen as the first step in the decline of Curtiss. The whole fleet flew some 3,750 flying time, and this aircraft was the worst failure of the US Navy of the pre-war era. 5-B-1 is Bu.No.9612 which replaced 9587 which stayed one week only at VB-5B. The other two are 9588/5-B-2 and 9589/5-B-3. (*SDAM*)

VB-5B
code: 5-B
November 1934 - February 1936

The BF2C-1 batch ordered was quickly delivered to the Navy and VB-5B became the unit chosen to operate this new fighter-bomber, receiving its first aircraft, and actually its full complement of 18 aircraft, in November 1934 (Bu.Nos 9588-9604, 9612). This unit was embarked on the latest aircraft-carrier of the USN, the USS *Ranger*. Soon afterwards, a major problem arose. While the metal-frame 'Hawk' wings gave full satisfaction on Army aircraft and the XF11C-3, the use of a different engine gave serious problems. Indeed, the natural period of vibration of the metal wings harmonised with the vibrations of the Cyclone engine, with the

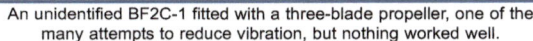

An unidentified BF2C-1 fitted with a three-blade propeller, one of the many attempts to reduce vibration, but nothing worked well.

result that the plane was close to breaking apart at cruising speed. Already by that time, one BF2C-1 (Bu.No 9594) had been lost for unknown causes on 29 January 1935, and the vibrations may have been an indirect cause of the crash, which killed the pilot. In the following months, the Navy tried to eliminate this problem, but could not fully achieve that. The only, and final, solution would have been to change the metal wings for the wooden-frame wings used on the successful Curtiss Hawk III, but this appeared too costly for the Navy. So after only one year of service, the Curtiss BF2C was withdrawn from use and VB-5B flew about 3,750 hours with their aircraft, some airframes totalling less than 5 hours. All the aircraft left the unit between October 1935 and February 1936, and all the surviving airframes (since Bu.No 9594 one BF2C had been lost on the ground, another during a test flight, and the last during its ferry flight to the storage facility) were stored before being stricken from the inventory on 1st February, 1937. A handful were kept for testing and surviving a couple of months more.

Compared to the 24,000 hours of the F11C/BFC fleet, which served longer in US Navy units, the disaster was total for Curtiss, who could not pretend after that date to remain a major fighter aircraft supplier for the Navy. As replacement, VB-5B received a batch of Boeing F4B-4s. When the BFC-2 landed for the last time, Curtiss had definitely lost the competition with Grumman, the latter maintaining its domination for the next forty years in supplying the best carrier-based fighters for the USN. In the next few years, Curtiss would develop four other prototypes of fighters but none saw production. The decline of Curtiss was slow but irreversible and had probably started with the failure of the BF2C.

The Register

Twenty-seven production aircraft F11C-3 ordered in February 1934 by contract 34906 (9586-9612). Delivered as BF2C-1.

9586

Del 07.10.34; Anacostia (bomb gear test); Dahlegren 19.10.34; Anacostia 22.10.34; NAF 19.11.34; Pratt & Whitney 03.01.35; Anacostia 20.02.35; Norfolk VX 27.02.35; Anacostia Pratt & Whitney 20.03.35; Anacostia 22.05.35; Curtiss 27.06.35; Norfolk (VX105) 29.06.35; Langley Field for vibration tests 28.10.35; Norfolk 05.12.35; Langley Field for vibration tests 06.02.36; Norfolk NAS awaiting strike-off 22.01.37. **Str-30.06.37** (105.7 TT).

9587

Del 24.10.34; Norfolk Battle Force then VB-5B USS *Ranger* 08.11.34; Norfolk Battle Force 15.11.34; san Diego Battle Force 19.03.35; VB-5B USS *Ranger* 02.04.35; San Diego 23.01.36; NAF 29.01.36; INA Curtiss 15.06.36; NAF for vibration tests 12.04.37 **Str-30.11.39.** (170.4 TT).

9588

Del 06.11.34; Norfolk Battle Force 13.11.34; VB-5B USS *Ranger* 10.11.34; San Diego Battle Force 18.04.35; VB-5B USS *Ranger* 28.08.35; San Diego Battle Force 30.10.35. **Str-01.02.37.** (74.4 TT)

9589

Del 06.11.34; Norfolk Battle Force 10.11.34; VF-5B USS *Ranger* 10.11.34; San Diego Battle Force 18.04.35; VB-5B USS Ranger 28.08.35; San Diego Battle Force 30.10.35. **Str-01.02.37.** (210.4 TT)

9590

Del 06.11.34; Norfolk Battle Force 07.11.34; VF-5B USS *Ranger* 07.11.34; San Diego Battle Force 03.10.35; NAF for structural tests 08.10.35. **Str-31.01.36.** (192.4 TT)

9591

Del 09.11.34; Norfolk Battle Force 10.11.34; VF-5B USS *Ranger* 10.11.34; San Diego Battle Force 20.10.35. **Str-01.02.37.** (164.2 TT)

9592

Del 08.11.34; Norfolk Battle Force 08.11.34; VF-5B USS *Ranger* 08.11.34.
On 17.08.35, at 15.00, a hangar sentry, Sea2c W.L. Elenton, USN, through carelessness, discharged a Very's pistol into the upper wing. The Very's atar ignited the fabric. The sentry did not notice the fire until it had gained considerable headway. The fire was extinguished by the use of extinguishers.
The aircraft was sent to San Diego Battle force on 23.08.35 for repairs, but it was found to badly damaged to consider any repairs and the aircraft was stricken from Navy inventory list. **Str-30.09.35.** (201.2 TT)

9593

Del 08.11.34; Norfolk Battle Force 08.11.34; VF-5B USS *Ranger* 08.11.34.
Crashed at sea on 11.09.35 19 miles coast at 10.35. No report was found, but local newspaper reported the death of his pilot, Walter Denison Leach, 33, 19 miles northwest off la Jolla (Los Angeles Times - 18 September 1935). **Str-31.10.345** (208.2 TT)

9594

Del 08.11.34; Norfolk Battle Force 08.11.34; VF-5B USS *Ranger* 08.11.34.
On 29.01.35, the pilot, Lt (jg) Robert C. Haven, USN, was flying a regularly authorised flight for the purpose of night section practice. He was flying in the number 3 position of the section led by Lt Teller, USN. The section was operating at about 6,000 feet over the assigned Virginia Beach area. The night was dark and clear, bright starlight with a light haze at 1,500 feet through which the ground lights showed clearly. Lt (jg) Reiner, USN, who was flying as number 2 position stated that several times during the early part of the flight, Lt (jg) Haven fell back in the formation as though about to leave but always rejoined shortly. About 19.00, he finally left the formation and seemed to be making flipper turns in the vicinity of the section and at the same altitude. The section leader turned to head for the home field and last saw the plane of Lt (jg) Haven circling in behind apparently to join up. As he pas-

Lemon Yellow cowling and fuselage band painted in yellow as well, outlined in black, identify the aircraft of the leader of the Sixth section. Note that the wheels seem to have been also painted in yellow, and if so, an unusual practice. Was it because it was an aircraft flown by a leader, was it a practice in force on the BF2C-1 fleet by the end of its career, it is not known. Bu.No 9602 was lost less than a year after it came into service while on a ferry flight to NAF to conduct one of the many vibration tests.
(National Archives)

Pilot of Bu.No 9588 coded 5-B-2, is about to start the engine for a routine flight over San Diego Bay. As second aircraft of the First section, the upper half cowling is painted in red. Note the absence of the Pegasus insignia, meaning that this photo was taken shortly after delivery to the USN. (National Archives)

Bu.No 9510 was not issued at first to VB-5B, being stored. Thus, it had a very short career as it arrived at VB-5B in July 1935 to become the second aircraft of the Third section with its upper half cowling painted in True blue, with a thin black line painted at its bottom. When stricken from the inventory, it had flown only 53 hours.
(National Archives)

23

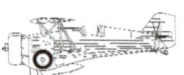

sed behind the section leader, Lt Teller lost sight of him because of the glare of the tail identification lights. Lt (jg) Haven's lights were all burning when last seen and he made no distress signal at any time. According to civilian witnesses, he crashed in the water of Linkhorn Bay near Virginia Beach shortly afterwards. Searching parties located the plane in twenty feet of water, late in the next afternoon. The condition of the plane and engine indicate that the plane hit the water in full flight with terrible force, apparently in dive of some sort.

The pilot who has logged about 1,000 flying hours, less than 30 on type, was killed. **Str-28.02.35**. (64.2 TT).

9595
Del 08.11.34; Norfolk Battle Force 13.11.34; VF-5B USS *Ranger* 16.11.34; San Diego Battle Force 16.04.35. **Str-01.02.37**. (64.2 TT)

9596
Del 08.11.34; Norfolk Battle Force then VF-5B USS *Ranger* 08.11.34; San Diego Battle Force 01.02.36. **Str-01.02.37**. (202.4 TT)

9597
Del 06.11.34; Norfolk Battle Force then VF-5B USS *Ranger* 08.11.34; San Diego Battle Force 30.10.35. **Str-01.02.37**. (212.3 TT)

9598
Del 09.11.34; Norfolk Battle Force then VF-5B USS *Ranger* 13.11.34; San Diego Battle Force 30.10.35. **Str-01.02.37**. (195.2 TT)

9599
Del 06.11.34; Norfolk Battle Force then VF-5B USS *Ranger* 08.11.34; San Diego Battle Force 26.02.36. **Str-01.02.37**. (193.6 TT)

9600
Del 08.11.34; Norfolk Battle Force then VF-5B USS *Ranger* 13.11.34; San Diego Battle Force 11.11.35. **Str-01.02.37**. (206.3 TT)

9601
Del 08.11.34; Norfolk Battle Force then VF-5B USS *Ranger* 08.11.34; San Diego Battle Force 05.11.35; NAF for vibration tests 11.11.35; INA Curtiss 18.08.36; NAF fro vibration tests 12.04.37. **Str-31.08.37**. (295.0 TT)

9602
Del 08.11.34; Norfolk Battle Force then VF-5B USS *Ranger* 08.11.34; San Diego Battle Force 24.10.35.

The pilot, Lt (jg.) W.C. Kaiser, USN, took off from Greensboro (NC) on 29.10.35 at 16.30 for Anacostia (DC), a distance of about 240 miles. Reported waether indicated conditions to be undesirable; overcast sky ceiling 2000-3000 feet with occasional showers. He attempted to land at Richmond but was prevented from doing so due to heavy rain. At 17.45 the ceiling had dropped to 400-500 feet. In lowering the wheels at this time the cord for the beacon receiver was carried away. Due to low ceiling, poor visibility, darkness, loss of use of the beacon receiver, and unfamiliarity with the surrounding country he became lost. In attempting to make a landing in a field at Manassas (VA) at 18.50, the plane struck a tree about 20 inches in diameter with the right wing. The engine was torn from the fuselage.

The pilot, who had over 1,100 hours logged sustained minor injuries, but the plane was not repaired. **Str-30.11.35**. (237.6 TT)

9603
Del 08.11.34; Norfolk Battle Force then VF-5B USS *Ranger* 13.11.34; San Diego Battle Force 19.08.35. **Str-01.02.37**. (165.4 TT)

9604
Del 08.11.34; Norfolk Battle Force then VF-5B USS *Ranger* 13.11.34; NAS Anacostia 11.01.35; VB-5B 28.01.35; San Diego Battle Force 05.08.35. **Str-01.02.37**. (163.0 TT)

9605
Del 12.11.34; Norfolk Battle Force 15.11.34; San Diego Battle Force 27.06.35; VB-5B USS *Ranger* 10.10.35; San Diego Battle Force 07.11.35. **Str-01.02.37**. (4.7 TT)

9606
Del 12.11.34; Norfolk Battle Force 15.11.34; San Diego Battle Force 19.03.35; VB-5B USS *Ranger* 08.04.35; San Diego Battle Force 30.10.35. **Str-01.02.37**. (133.0 TT)

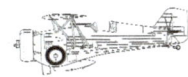

9607
Del 12.11.34; Norfolk Battle Force 15.11.34; San Diego Battle Force 19.03.35; VB-5B USS *Ranger* 01.04.35; San Diego Battle Force 26.02.36. **Str-01.02.37**. (105.4 TT)

9608
Del 12.11.34; Norfolk Battle Force 15.11.34; San Diego Battle Force 27.06.35; VB-5B USS *Ranger* 16.08.35; San Diego Battle Force 29.01.36. **Str-01.02.37**. (20.5 TT)

9609
Del 12.11.34; Norfolk Battle Force 15.11.34; San Diego Battle Force 27.06.35. **Str-01.02.37**. (4.7 TT)

9610
Del 12.11.34; Norfolk Battle Force 15.11.34; San Diego Battle Force 27.06.35; VB-5B USS *Ranger* 12.07.35; San Diego Battle Force 30.01.36. **Str-01.02.37**. (53.2 TT)

9611
Del 12.11.34; VB-5B USS *Ranger* 05.02.35; San Diego Battle Force 18.07.35. **Str-01.02.37**. (115.8 TT)

9612
Del 12.11.34; VB-5B USS *Ranger* 15.11.34; San Diego Battle Force 18.04.35; VB-5B 06.08.35; San Diego Battle Force 26.02.36. **Str-01.02.37**. (112.9 TT)

Roll of Honour

Curtiss F11C, BFC, BF2C

Name	Rank	Origin	Date	BuNo
ARTHUR, W.S.	Lt (jg)	USN	12.12.33	9268
BOADWEE, H.N.	Lt	USNR	04.05.36	9340
HAVEN, R.C.	Ens.	USN	09.01.35	9594
LEACH, W.D.	Lt (jg)	USN	11.09.35	9395
PALMER, K.P.	Lt	USN	16.09.35	9280

Total: 5

Bu.No 9596 pictured taxiing was the aircraft of the leader of the Fourth section, with its usual black colour (fuselage band and cowling – see colour profile).

Another side view of Bu.No 9588 with its engine warming up. The retractable landing gear was rather new for US Navy aircraft, however a concept introduced by Grumman with its FF-1, a two-seat fighter. During the first half of the thirties, US Navy was experiencing new concepts, like the fighter-bomber, retractable landing gear or two-seat fighters, with varying results. (*National Archives*)

Opposite side view of a BF2C-1, this time Bu.No 9601, coded 5-B-15, meaning that it is the third aircraft of the Fifth Section, identified with its Willow Green colour. Here too, the wheels seems to be painted, but not in green. (*National Archives*)

The Fourth Section of VB-5B embarked on USS *Ranger* as it should appear in flight in 1934-1935. The Fourth Section was identified by its black colour, with Bu.No 9596/5-B-10, Bu.No 9597/5-B-11 and Bu.No 9598/5-B-12. The chevron painted on the upper wings were painted in the normal position (see F11C-2 plate).

Squadron Section Colours

First (Insignia Red)	Third (True Blue)	Fifth (Willow Green)
Aircraft #1, #2, #3	Aircraft #7, #8, #9	Aircraft #13, #14, #15

Second (White)	Fourth (Black)	Sixth (Lemon Yellow)
Aircraft #4, #5, #6	Aircraft #10, #11, #12	Aircraft #16, #17, #18

(Aircraft of the leaders (#1, 4, 7, 10, 13, 16) were also identified with a fuselage band painted at the colour of the Section

www.ingramcontent.com/pod-product-compliance
Lightning Source LLC
Chambersburg PA
CBHW060803090426
42736CB00002B/140